Little Princess Rani and the Pala

Rani Celebrates Holi

By Anita Badhwar

For Vikram and Divya

Thank you to Mom, Dad, and Anil for your support

ISBN-13: 978-1505549409

Rani is a little Princess of a Kingdom in India. Rani has

a pet parrot named Hari.

One evening, Princess Rani, Hari, and Rani's lady-in-waiting, Jaya, were playing soccer in the palace's royal garden. "Tomorrow we will be celebrating *Holi*, the spring festival of colors, with our citizens," said Rani excitedly. "Holi! Holi!" squawked Hari.

"It is going to be so much fun!" said Jaya. "That's right, Jaya. Holi is always fun because as part of the festivities we get to throw *gulal* (colored powder) on each other to celebrate the arrival of spring," said Rani. It was almost time for dinner, so they began their walk back to the palace.

Along their walk, they met Rani's pet elephant Bindi. "*Namaste* (greetings) Princess Rani," said Bindi. "Namaste, Bindi. We were just talking about how we are going to celebrate the festival of Holi tomorrow," said Rani. "Yes, and we are going to get SOOOOOO messy!" added Jaya. "Messy! Messy!" squawked Hari.

"How will we be celebrating?" asked Bindi. "We'll throw gulal and water balloons filled with colored water at each other. Then we'll have fun spraying each other with colored water using *pichkaris* (water guns)," replied Rani. "Princess Rani, we should go, it's time for dinner," reminded Jaya. "Gotta go, Bindi, we'll see you tomorrow," said Rani.

After they left, Bindi was worried. "MESSY?" Bindi thought to herself. She did not like the idea of getting messy. NOT AT ALL. "I'm a very clean elephant. When I eat I always make sure I wipe my mouth with my napkin," she thought to herself.

"When I get muddy from playing outside, I always wash my feet. At night, I always make sure that I brush my teeth. What am I going to do?" thought Bindi as she walked towards the palace.

Bindi ended up in the palace's royal courtyard. She stared at the buckets of gulal and the pichkaris. There were colors of *laal* (red), *hara* (green), *neela* (blue), *jamuni* (purple) and many more!

Suddenly, Bindi had an idea. Bindi decided that she would hide all the buckets of gulal! "If there is no gulal, then there will be no mess!"Bindi thought to herself.

So that night, while everyone was asleep, Bindi hid all the buckets of gulal.

The next morning, Rani, Jaya, and Hari were walking through the royal courtyard when they met the palace's Royal Decorator. He looked upset. "Princess Rani, yesterday the buckets of gulal were ready for today's Holi celebration, but this morning, I see that they are all missing!" he said.

"OH NO!" exclaimed Rani. "We can't celebrate Holi without gulal!" said Jaya sadly. "Maybe the buckets are around here somewhere. Let's search the palace to try and find them," suggested Rani."Let's go! Let's go!" squawked Hari.

While Rani, Jaya, and Hari were searching for the buckets, Bindi was taking her usual morning walk through the kingdom. She noticed that all the citizens were sad. They had found out that there may not be a Holi celebration this year because the buckets of gulal had gone missing.

Bindi felt terrible. She had made a big mistake. "Everyone is sad because of me. How can I make everyone happy again?" she thought to herself. As Bindi walked back to the palace, she decided that she would tell Rani about what she had done. "Princess Rani will know what to do," thought Bindi.

Bindi found Rani outside. "Princess Rani, I have something to tell you. I hid all the buckets of gulal," said Bindi. "Oh no, Bindi! But why?" asked Rani. "When we were talking about Holi yesterday, Jaya and Hari said that it was going to be really messy," said Bindi.

"Princess Rani, I'm a very clean elephant. I don't like to get messy, which is why I hid all the buckets of gulal,"explained Bindi. "But on my walk this morning, I saw that all the citizens were very sad after finding out that there may not be a Holi celebration this year," she said.

"That made me feel awful for what I did," said Bindi. "But Bindi, Holi is the one festival when you are SUPPOSED to get messy!" exclaimed Rani. "Really?" asked Bindi. "Yes Bindi! It is going to be lots and lots of fun!" said Rani. "Well, I don't know..." said Bindi doubtfully. Then Rani had an idea that would certainly

change Bindi's mind. "Bindi, I have a special job for you during the Holi celebration," said Rani. "You do?" asked Bindi. After telling Bindi about her special job, Bindi agreed immediately to take part in the celebration. "Now let's return all the buckets of gulal so that we can all happily celebrate Holi today!" said Rani. "Let's go!" said Bindi.

As soon as the buckets of gulal were returned, the Royal Decorator took some of it to make colored water for the water balloons and pichkaris. The citizens began to arrive in the palace's royal garden. Rani's mother, the *Maharani* (Great Queen),

her father, the *Maharaja* (Great King), and her brother Raja, all welcomed the citizens.

Everyone changed into traditional Indian white clothing, so that the Holi colors will

be visible. They were all happy and ready to celebrate Holi, especially Bindi!

First, everyone began to throw the gulal everywhere and on each other!

Bindi began to throw gulal with her trunk too!

Next, they began throwing the water ballooons!

POP!

POP!

POP!

Hari and Bindi tossed water balloons too!

Then everyone picked up a pichkari and sprayed each other with colored water!

Once all the Holi fun was over, it was time for Bindi's special job...

Bindi dunked her trunk in a big bucket of water and splashed everyone CLEAN with water! "Princess Rani, you were right. I had so much fun getting messy in the Holi celebration today! But the best part of the celebration is getting all cleaned up!" said Bindi with a smile on her face.

SPLASH!

At the end of the day, Rani had dinner, said goodnight to Bindi and went to her royal bedroom with Hari. Rani was happy that Bindi returned the gulal and enjoyed the Holi celebration with everyone. She fell asleep dreaming about the Holi fun and all the beautiful colors of spring!

The Meaning of Holi

Holi, the spring festival of colors, is celebrated all over the world. It is believed that the throwing of *gulal* (colored powder) originated with the Hindu God, Krishna. Thus, in the city of Mathura (Lord Krishna's birthplace) and in Vrindavan, (where he grew up), Holi is celebrated in an extravagant manner each spring.

The origin of the festival's name can be traced back to a story about a boy named Prahlad. Prahlad's father, King Hiranyakashyap was a tyrant, who wanted everyone in his kingdom to worship him as God. Prahlad instead worshipped the Hindu God, Vishnu, which angered his father. As a result, the King tried to slay Prahlad many times, but failed. The King decided to asked his sister, Holika, for help. Holika had a special blessing which protected her from fire. Using this special blessing, he devised a plan in which Holika would trick Prahlad into allowing her to hold him while she walked through a fire in order to slay him. After entering the fire, Holika perished, not Prahlad. It is believed that the blessing worked on Holika alone, and that Lord Vishnu intervened to save Prahlad because of his devotion to him. On the night before Holi, people light bonfires which symbolize the burning of Holika. Thus, Holi is a celebration of the victory of good over evil.

Made in the USA
Lexington, KY
24 December 2017